FOREWORD

As we scour the globe for new luxury indulgences and unique experiences, "proximity to a spa" has become a major, if not *the* major consideration when choosing a lavish escape. In recognition of this, luxury publishers, The Best 100: have gathered together a superior collection of outstanding spas from the African continent. Whether Resort Spa, Bush Spa, Destination Spa or Day Spa, Africa enjoys a thriving culture of wellness, providing sophisticated spa seekers with a wealth of choice. In your search for the ultimate indulgence, The Best 100: offers you a peek behind the doors of some of the most glamorous spas in Africa.

Let the pampering begin.

Image courtesy of Etali Safari Lodge

AFRICA BOASTS A RICH SPA CULTURE with some of the most innovative, cleverly designed and cutting-edge spas in the world. Impeccably trained therapists offer an enviable range of treatments and rituals whether for healing or pampering; using the world's favourite branded spa products alongside more traditional African treatments.

Set in some of the most sensational locations amid breathtaking scenery, you can find yourself being massaged while overlooking the azure-blue waters of the Indian Ocean, aside Table Mountain or surrounded by the heaving sound of nature; a crocodile or rhino lazily basking outside your Bush Spa. Using modern state-of-the-art technology and a hybrid of modern and ancient techniques, African spas are at the forefront of the spa revolution.

Enjoy.

spas in Africa

CONTENTS

RESORT SPAS

BUSH SPAS

IOO:

CONTENTS

DESTINATION SPAS

DAY SPAS

RESORT SPA

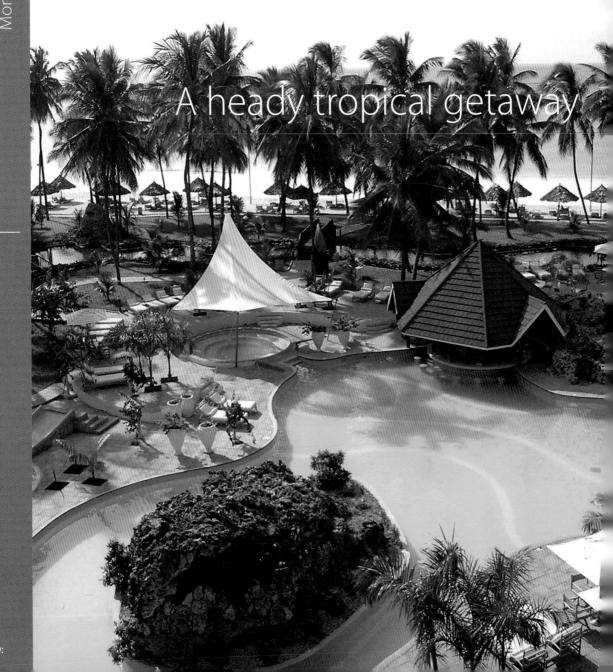

A heady tropical getaway

Along Kenya's coast, tucked away in the midst of palm fronds, sits the Diani Reef Beach Resort & Spa, a luxurious getaway for the discerning traveler. Everything about this huge property promises what every weary traveler requires the most – rest, rejuvenation and relaxation. On one side of the resort, shimmering turquoise waters of the Indian Ocean caress the pristine white sands of endless beach, on the other; immaculate landscaping exudes a heady tropical atmosphere.

The spa menu reads like an exotic journey through a wide-spectrum of holistic therapies

DIANI REEF'S "MAYA" SPA IS ONE OF THE finest spas in the country and takes an uncompromising approach to health, well-being and beauty. This goes well beyond appearance to treat, touch, scent and surround every part of you. All the therapies offered at Maya have been carefully chosen to create the perfect environment in combating stress, pollution and discomforts caused by urban life. Maya is committed to holistic health and has selected ingredients that are as close to nature as possible. Dedicated professional staff will help and advise on a variety of personalised face and body treatments designed to make your stay as memorable as possible.

Exotic Journey

The spa menu reads like an exotic journey capturing the healing energy emanating from a wide spectrum of holistic therapies. Ayurveda, Thallaso Therapy, Balenotherapy, Aqua or Hydro Treatment, Reflexology, Aromatherapy, Body and Face treatments, will all soothe your soul. Yoga, Aerobics, Meditation and Salon Services make Maya spa a unique destination rather than an "ordinary spa" experience – a tranquil balance of nature soothing stress and easing strain.

All Touch Therapies begin with a Floral Foot Wash Ritual, a ceremony symbolising a cleansing of the soul. After the treatment, linger in our relaxation garden and enjoy a Herbal Tea Celebration. With today's pace of life becoming increasingly demanding and stressful, more and more of us are seeking a sanctuary into which we can escape. Although touch therapies and massages have been around for centuries, never before has the quest for wellness and harmony been so great. §

The jewel in the crown

A jewel in the crown of Moroccan hospitality, at La Sultana, whatever the time or season, all senses are inspired. Everything is possible, everywhere and at every moment – it is the supreme pinnacle of luxurious hospitality. Clasped like a priceless diamond in the city walls.

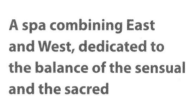

A spa combining East and West, dedicated to the balance of the sensual and the sacred

IN THE SPACIOUS SPA AREA, THE JADE COLOUR of the corridors suggest the aquatic. Walls and ceiling turn into an ocean. And then, when the two sides of the Indian doorway open – a surprise! An immense universe punctuated with elegant and powerful Roman pillars rising from an ancient basin and reaching out into vaults and echoing domes.

All sense of time and place is lost in total harmony, the sounds, scents and light of the country mingle. There are communal and private hammams, saunas, jacuzzi, massage parlours, resting rooms and other delightful spots. The latest techniques of the Western world – Balneotherapy, Aromatherapy, Algotherapy, Chromotherapy – complement a selection of age-old treatments.

Clasped like a jewel in the city walls, La Sultana boasts a terrace of 1 200m². As in the time of Babylon, this hanging garden symbolises the supreme sophistication of the Sultana. What do we gaze at first? The scented drapes of bougainvillea, coloured mother-of-pearl or flaming ruby? Or the elegant architecture of the Koutoubia? The legendary chain of the Atlas mountains; its snow-capped crests unfurled into the distance?

A nation's cuisine reveals its cultural achievements. In this area, Morocco is indeed a kingdom; the Moroccan chef fuses French cuisine with the exotic. Be caressed by the first rays of the sun, enjoying breakfast by the swimming pool or the terrace, lulled by a concert of birds in the flowering bushes. Be massaged in the open air, take a dip in the refreshing pool or be attended to on the terrace.

La Sultana is the perfect place to inform, unite, motivate, perpetuate, succeed. Perfect for management meetings, seminars, conferences. The exceptional setting will give birth to a great event. §

Make contact
see directory page 92

13:

French chic in a stunning
tropical environment

One of the world's truly romantic resorts set on a beautiful stretch of white-beach – Le Touessrok is the essence of cool, modern elegance, imbued by the cultural warmth of tropical Mauritius. Across the water are two exquisite islands, including the spectacular championship golf course by Bernhard Langer and the private retreat island Ilot Mangénie.

THIS IS A HAVEN OF LUXURY where every whim is catered for. The Givenchy Spa on the adjacent Frangipani Island, provides wonderful treatments for body and spirit and occupies a world of its own. Unlike many care institutes around the world, the Givenchy Spa concept is exclusive and there are only a handful of Givenchy Spas in the world, as chosen locations must be 'magical'.

Cool, modern elegance, imbued by the cultural warmth of tropical Mauritius

During the signature four-hand Ylang-Ylang Massage the guest relaxes on a heated table, with gentle music in the background, succumbing to the luxury as two therapists, trained to work in tandem, do a mirror-imaged massage on both halves of the body.

The stones used for the Canyon Love Stone Therapy are from Arizona rivers and have extended heat-retaining properties. They provide a warm, relaxing massage which balances energies while working on the chakras, detoxifying tissues and relieving muscular tension, inducing a calm state of mind.

There is a state-of-the-art Fitness Centre, whose personal trainers work in close conjunction with the spa team; a boutique selling Givenchy products and the Hairdressing Salon, where hairstyling can be combined with manicures and pedicures.

Le Touessrok really does have it all. The experience is unique. 🙎

Make contact
see directory page 92

15:

Sensual sophistication
sumptuous surroundings

Soaring above the glittering Knysna lagoon, Pezula offers breathtaking mountain and ocean views; overlooking a lush nature reserve, while encompassing the exquisite sheltered beach at nearby Noetzie. The exquisite spa is steeped in total luxury.

There is an atmosphere of unhurried calm as the staff cosset guests with service and attention

INSIDE THIS REMARKABLE RESORT HOTEL, there is an atmosphere of unhurried calm as the staff cosset guests with service and attention. There's the sensuous pampering of a health spa, gourmet meals lovingly prepared from the freshest local ingredients, and the delightful seclusion of your suite with its own private balcony. Highly personalised service is the hallmark of the Pezula Resort.

It nestles in its own golf estate on an exclusive cliff-top retreat, surrounded by an aromatic mantle of Cape coastal fynbos – bushes, trees and wild flowers teeming with birds and insects.

Health spa

Light and airy, the Health Spa is a multi award-winning state-of-the-art spa that offers customised facial and body treatments, and massage therapy. There's a gym, indoor pool and access to all of Pezula's sporting facilities, while Knysna and its surrounds provide an abundance of outdoor activities. Let the spa come to you and luxuriate in a massage or aromatherapy session on your own private balcony.

Invigorated by this care, you may choose to take advantage of Pezula's extensive sport and recreation facilities, ranging from envigorating nature walks to yachting, diving and more. Pezula is the finest combination imaginable: secluded sophistication and breathtaking natural perfection.

Fine dining

Cape Rock lobster, Knysna oysters and freshly-caught line fish are a few of the local delights prepared by Pezula's master chef. He begins with the very finest and freshest local ingredients in season, insisting on organically grown produce. He then prepares each dish to bring out the full natural flavours and enhance succulence and tenderness.

The result is a gourmet menu that is simple yet deeply satisfying, combined with some of the finest Cape and international vintages.

GOLF COURSE: The championship golf course lies high above the heaving Indian Ocean and the vast Knysna lagoon – a sweeping spectacle of fairways and greens rolling through the pristine indigenous landscape.

TREAT: The Pezula private jet and helicopter are available for charter. A chauffeur and limousine service is available for trips into town and surrounds. §

Make contact
see directory page 92

Peace and tranquillity
in lush tropical gardens

Preskîl, meaning 'peninsula' in French, is a haven of peace and tranquillity set in over three hectares of lush tropical garden on a private peninsula. The stunning architecture of this newly-renovated resort was inspired by typical Creole homes and the original colonial houses built on Mauritius by early settlers.

Long lazy strolls along the beach make it a wonderfully romantic and relaxing destination

ASIDE FROM A LONG IDYLLIC WHITE SANDY BEACH, Preskîl, a 4-star hotel, overlooks the Island's largest lagoon, and is close to the magnificent Blue Bay Marine Park and l'Ile aux Aigrettes bird sanctuary. Blue Bay offers exceptional diving and beautiful unspoilt beaches.

Spa and wellness

The warmth of the tropical sun and the joys of the sea conspire to make an unforgettable relaxing trip and its modern and well-equipped wellness centre will relax guests further. A team of dedicated professionals is ready to introduce you to the delight of being pampered by indulging in a range of body care and massages. Preskîl's spa has 5 individual massage rooms + 2 duo massage rooms with a Japanese bath + 1 body wrapping room + 2 hammams, and a fitness gym for a good work-out after a hot day in the sun.

The one core value on which Preskîl Beach Resort has based its entire philosophy, is that "service is gold". From warm welcomes to personalised advice, Preskîl Beach Resort staff pride themselves on their service record and are dedicated to making guests feel as comfortable as possible.

Despite the fact that this is a large resort, the setting makes it a wonderfully romantic and relaxing destination and its relative isolation allows for long lazy strolls along the beach and easy avoidance of the hustle and bustle of typical resort activity, although it's there if you want it.

The warmth and authenticity of the Mauritian people is the key to an unforgettable break in an exceptional environment where relaxation and amusement come easily. §

Make contact
see directory page 92

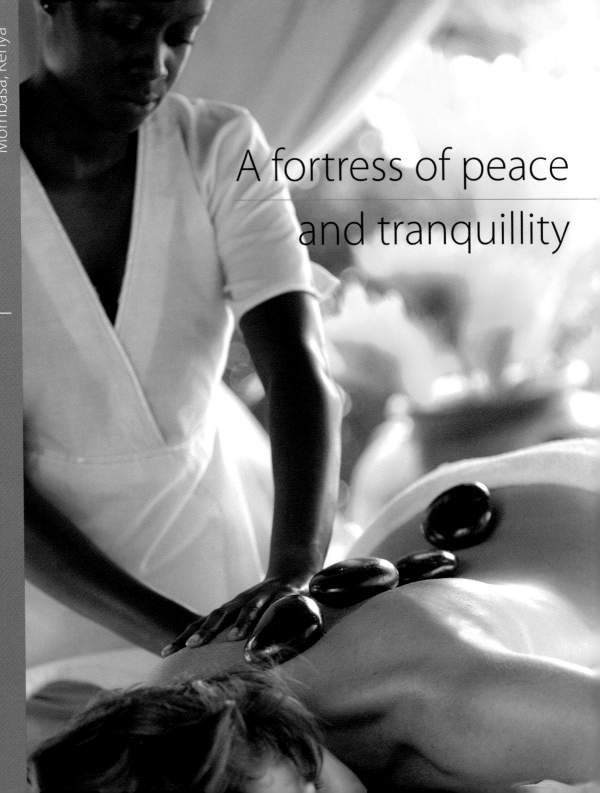

A fortress of peace
and tranquillity

In a world of shrinking time and stress impact, the need for inner peace is critical. The Serena Maisha Spa is a sanctuary of calm that draws on the beauty of nature, leaving guests refreshed and rejuvenated.

A sanctuary of calm that draws on the beauty of nature, and the elation of evocative surroundings

THE SERENA MAISHA SPA IS ONLY ONE of three establishments in Africa to belong to the respected, International Spa Association, which sets the standards for global compliance with authentic spa practices. It's a place to rejuvenate, cleanse and polish your body to perfection with unique body exfoliation and invigoration routines, utilising nature-based body rubs and ultra-nourishing body wraps to make your skin glow with health.

Their treatment range is as holistic as their concept. Choose from energising 'hot-stone' massages in the style of the ancient Maya civilisation, luxuriant nature-based body wraps and 'body glows'; a stunning range of Ionothermine slimming, anti-cellulite and face-and-body-shaping regimes.

TREAT: Try an Andean hot stone therapy; the ultimate spa treatment that massages and caresses your entire body, leaving you in a state of deep relaxation and calm. ⁸

An exotic
favourite gets
a welcome
facelift

A priceless gem situated on the West Coast of Mauritius. The Sofitel Imperial sparkles amid nine hectares of lush tropical gardens, fringed by several kilometres of beautiful white sandy beaches and an emerald lagoon.

Providing guests with the ultimate luxury of the best nature has to offer

DURING 2007, IN A PERMANENT QUEST FOR EXCELLENCE, the Sofitel Imperial undertook a total renovation, modernising 143 of its rooms and suites. Together with its newly-designed restaurant, lobby and Kestrel bar and a 1000m² cutting-edge Spa; one of the most famous in Mauritius and with its fitness centre overlooking the garden and lake, the Sofitel Imperial Hotel is now among the Top 10 hotels in Mauritius. The refurbishment was carried out by an international Interior designer who has designed a fresh, open-plan layout for the rooms.

The elegance of the lines and the richness of the woods combine with pastel ambiances to offer guests a very enriching experience. The new elegant rooms are extremely welcoming and comfortable.

New spa

At Le Spa the Oriental influence can be felt everywhere with treatments based on exotic fruits, spices and flowers. Experience a feeling of total relaxation in every muscle. Take time out to recharge your batteries, since this is what the spa aims for – to help guests restore equilibrium, invigorating the senses and refreshing the spirit with new energy. Providing guests with the ultimate luxury of the best nature has to offer. Spa highlights include; Imperial Lulur, an age-old treatment undertaken by a bride and groom to beautify the skin before the wedding celebrations; Earth of Mauritius, a body scrub with Mauritian

salts followed by a body pack of fresh pineapple, papaya, lemon and honey.

Enjoy international buffets at the Ravinala restaurant or gourmet cuisine at the Jacaranda beach restaurant. One may sample Chinese specialities at the Ming Court restaurant or experience Japanese demonstrative cuisine at the Teppanyaki tables. Local cuisine is also served at the Tamassa beach restaurant for light lunches. §

Make contact
see directory page 92

SOFITEL IMPERIAL MAURITIUS

Impeccable service,
outstanding cuisine
and uber-chic design

Situated in the middle of one of the largest lagoons in the Maldives, the Taj Exotica Resort and Spa, blends seamlessly with the idyllic beauty of this tropical isle.

SINCE IT OPENED, TAJ EXOTICA RESORT AND SPA, Maldives has attracted prestigious awards from leading publications around the globe such as Condé Nast Traveller's "Hot list" and Harpers & Queen's "Resort of the Year", with press acclaim focusing on impeccable service, an elevated degree of care and outstanding cuisine, combined with uber-chic design. The Taj has since taken this feedback and improved on it by reducing the number of villas on the island to offer un-rivelled privacy and luxury in the middle of the ocean. Settling on 62 spacious palm-thatched villas ranging from Lagoon Villas to the magnificent 450m^2 Rehendi Presidential suite.

The first contemporary Indian spa to open outside of India

Taj Spa

The Taj Spa opened in 2006 as the first authentic Indian spa to be experienced outside of India and was designed in conjunction with a Vastushastra Master (India's answer to Feng Shui). Energy earth readings have been meticulously combined with ancient Indian space-clearing principles to create the perfect environment for relaxation and rejuvenation. Guests can indulge in Indian, Royal and holistic experiences; treatments and ceremonies especially designed to maintain physical, mental and spiritual equilibrium in life. The concept is rooted in the belief that a spa is more than four walls and a treatment room, it is a way of life; which is integral to the Indian philosophy of wellness.

Signature Taj Treatments, Indian Royal beauty rituals, body therapies and authentic in-depth Ayurveda programmes can be enjoyed at the signature Indian Royal Mud and Bathing Experience Pavilion, the Ayurveda Sanctuary Pavilion or the Heat, Hydro and Relaxation Experience Pavilion. Guest can also experience unique Spa cuisine including a range of regenerative, anti-oxidant and 'Satvik' dishes (based on the Ayurvedic principles). §

A luxurious
haven of solitude

Enveloped by mountains and encircling a stunning lagoon, this luxurious haven of solitude on one of the most beautiful beaches in Mauritius is the last word in luxury.

OVERLOOKING TAMARIN BAY, TAJ EXOTICA RESORT & SPA, Mauritius has 65 villas each providing the utmost privacy with a view of the sea, individual plunge pool and al-fresco dining-living area.

Large and spacious, the villas offer all luxury features like satellite television, digital videodisc player, a music system, a surround television system, international dialing to high-speed and wireless internet.

The spa features a Yoga-meditation Pavilion, with regular sessions conducted by trained instructors

Indian-inspired Taj Spa

A unique feature at the resort is its top-of-the-line Taj Spa that offers a range of Indian-inspired signature treatments from deep muscular massages and relaxation Aromatherapy to detoxification cleansing wraps and Ayurvedic applications that pamper the senses. The spa also features a Yoga-meditation Pavilion, with regular sessions conducted by passionate instructors and healers.

The fully-equipped sports centre, floodlit tennis court, large swimming pool, range of water sports and challenging golf course complete the holiday experience.

Cuisine

Apart from the in-villa dining, this resort spa offers an eclectic dining experience with all-day casual dining at the *Coast2Coast* restaurant, serving Mediterranean, International and Creole cuisine. Fine dining at the *Cilantro* speciality restaurant features a cross-section of Pan Asian/ Japanese cuisine and a variety of the rich flavours of India.

CHILDREN WELCOME: The Taj Exotica Resort and Spa, Mauritius is an ideal destination for families with children; a special Kids' Club offers a complete range of amenities and services to enhance a young traveler's holiday experience.

Make contact
see directory page 92

BUSH SPA

Place of new beginnings

Out of the heart of the spectacular Madikwe Game Reserve, embraced by pristine bushveld, Etali Safari Lodge rises to meet you with lavish hospitality. Etali, meaning 'a new beginning' respects the privacy of guests while offering impeccable personal attention.

Etali's unique concept allows you to discover how fantastically good you really can feel

ETALI'S CORE HOLISTIC PHILOSOPHY OF natural health incorporates the healing and rejuvenation of body, mind and spirit. The state-of-the-art Wellness Centre is a unique concept that allows you to discover how fantastically good you really can feel.

Enjoy a massage on your own sundeck – therapeutic in itself – or relax in the caring hands of qualified therapists in one of the treatment rooms overlooking the savannah. The Aromatherapy massages, Indian head massage, hot-stone therapy, body-wraps and facials provide for an exciting and exotic journey. The mini-gym facilities offer a more energetic contrast.

Game Safari

Share the exciting unpredictability of an early-morning game drive with an expert ranger or take a walk through the bush. Madikwe has over 300 species of birds. Africa's "Big Five", the African wild dog, black and white rhino, cheetah, giraffe and many other glorious species sashay across the Madikwe Plains. Guides will explain the medicinal value of trees and plants, and delight with stories of the magical powers attributed to them.

Etali's delectable cuisine is a contemporary fusion of traditional African with an Asian twist. Meals are light and healthy with lots of fresh seasonal and organically-grown vegetables, fruit and herbs. There is no set menu as the chef "extraordinaire" selects only local produce daily. Fine wine from the Cape's boutique estates tempt your palate.

Madikwe portrays eco-tourism at its best. These 75 000 hectares of malaria-free splendour are part of a conservation partnership. 🔆

Make contact
see directory page 92

Falaza Game Park & Spa
KwaZulu-Natal, South Africa

Sense-soothing
body safaris

Situated in Hluhluwe, overlooking Lake St Lucia and False Bay, central to major game reserves and Zulu cultural villages, Falaza Game Park and Spa is the perfect escape from the hustle and bustle of everyday life.

Relax and rejuvenate in game park splendor under African skies

ULTIMATE PHYSICAL AND MENTAL relaxation awaits you at the Falaza Spa, which is nestled among our tranquil, indigenous gardens, often visited by game from the reserve. Specialised treatments, making use of internationally-renowned Thalgo and TheraNaka products, create a sublime sense of release for both men and women alike.

From traditionally-inspired foot cleansing, to a full range of massages and holistic spa treatments, Falaza's innovative spa offers pampering, sense-soothing body safaris. After time spent in the African bush, nothing is better suited to combining relaxation with hydration and gentle cleansing.

Prior to treatments guests are taken to a relaxation area for a traditional Falaza Foot cleanse, where the feet are bathed in a bowl of warm water with a blend of essential oils… the perfect start to a session of luxurious pampering.

Indulgent spa packages range from half day treatments to the five-day premier spa experience – combining heavenly treatments, candle-lit dinners and bubbling spa baths, three tasty meals each day, safari experiences and luxury tented accommodation, all of which combine to make Falaza the ultimate safari spa destination. §

Make contact
see directory page 92

Safari for the soul

Garonga is an exclusive 14-bed tented Safari camp west of the Kruger National Park. This unassuming sanctuary delivers an intimate wildlife encounter in an unhurried environment with the opportunity for spectacular game viewing.

Invigorating outdoor bush-baths combined with aromatherapy and reflexology sessions are available at the Bush Spa

TENTED ROOMS ARE SET ON A DRY RIVERBED – each with a wooden deck commanding spectacular views. Textured earthy colours and clean lines set off with fine linen and luxury accessories ensure pure comfort. The camp's holistic philosophy is to offer a "safari for the soul", allowing time to reflect and find inspiration in the nature that surrounds. Guests can either join in every activity on offer or laze around in a hammock with a good book while watching grazing impala.

Bundu-bashing game drives, wilderness walks, and under-the-stars sleep overs allow guests to walk close to the animals, enhancing the whole wildlife encounter. But it isn't all heat and dust.

Invigorating outdoor bush-baths combined with aromatherapy and reflexology sessions are available at the Bush Spa. Expert therapists will soothe away urban stresses with Indian Head Massage and Hot Stone Therapy leading their speciality list. Their signature Honeymoon Couple Instructional Massage is certainly worth a try whether you're "just married" or not.

MUST TRY: The Hambleden Suite is very private and super-luxurious. An ebony four-poster bed with en-suite bathroom includes a charming hand-beaten copper bath and matching basins. The private pool and deck add that special touch. The cuisine at Garonga Safari Camp is a fusion of the resident chef's culinary skills, matched to excellent South African wines. §

Make contact
see directory page 92

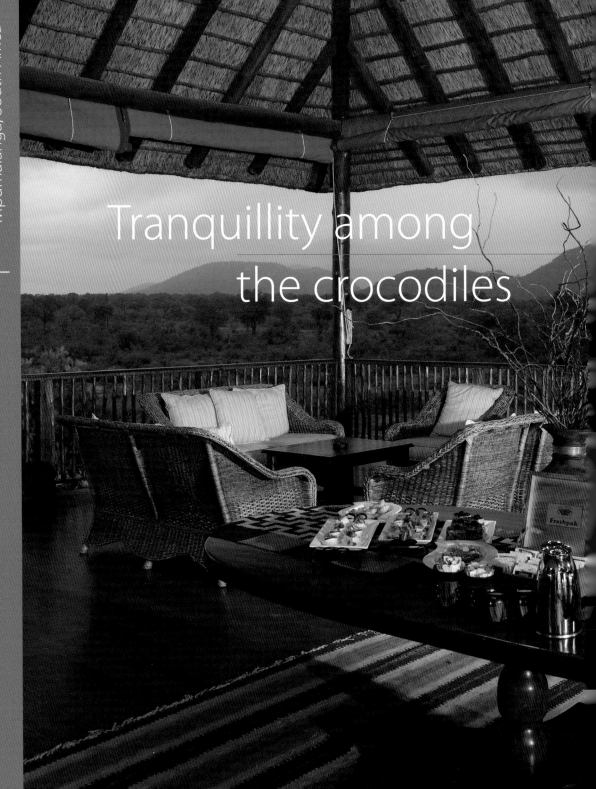

Tranquillity among
the crocodiles

Located on the Nkomazi Tourist Route – "The Wild Frontier" – in Mpumalanga, Pestana Kruger Lodge is just 150 metres from the most important entrance to the south side of the Kruger National Park – Malelane Gate. The lodge and spa are set among exquisite gardens and have a fantastic view over the Crocodile River where hippos and other wildlife abound. It is a wonderfully relaxing location where you will scarcely hear the animals yet be surrounded by nature.

A truly unique setting surrounded by nature, including the "Big 5"

THE KRUGER NATIONAL PARK has almost 2,000 km of roads and six permanent rivers that cross the savannah within the park. It is the habitat of countless species including the "Big 5" – Lion, Leopard, Elephant, Buffalo and Rhinoceros; plus 336 types of tree, 49 species of fish, 114 types of reptiles and 507 species of birds, and innumerable giraffe, monkeys, zebras and antelopes.

It is a truly unique setting with a magnificent view over the river and luxuriant vegetation where game can be viewed while dining. The restaurant is located over the water inhabited by crocodiles. Sip an exotic cocktail while watching the sunset, in the bar or view deck while the game come to drink at the Crocodile River.

Health spa

Camelot Spa at Pestana Kruger Lodge is unique, luxurious and fully-equipped with a hydro bath, steam room, relaxation area and a double treatment suite which leads out onto its own private treatment garden. The experience of a bush massage will bring your body back to life with the tranquillity of the bushveld and the healing touch of your therapist.

Combine this with Camelot's philosophy of creating a haven to relax and revitalise your body, mind and soul, and you will have the experience of a lifetime. A healthy but tasty Spa menu is available, to tempt the taste buds while brimming with good nutrition. §

Make contact
see directory page 92

Wild, untamed setting,
epic indulgence

Internationally renowned for providing the pinnacle of luxury game viewing, this regal getaway is now home to one of the most exclusive spas on the continent.

COMPLETELY SURROUNDED by the untamed African Bush, the Waters of Royal Malawane Bush Spa is a veritable oasis of calm. Internationally qualified therapists are on hand to provide a luxurious range of massages, body treatments and hydrotherapy treatments. This is the ultimate refuge for those seeking to refresh mind, body and spirit.

The Spa's philosophy draws on the healing powers of water and all hydrotherapy treatments use untainted, mineral-rich water sourced from an underground stream that flows through the reserve. Filtered through limestone and granite, these are the very waters this incomparable Bush Spa takes its name from.

Defining the African experience are a selection of completely unique and unashamedly indulgent signature treatments using rare indigenous oils and traditional ingredients, providing a sensory experience with an

Unique and unashamedly indulgent signature treatments use rare indigenous oils and traditional ingredients

unforgettable African touch. Stretching out majestically between gnarled Jackelberry and Acacia Thorn, the Bush Spa's clean lines and minimalistic design exude an air of complete balance and tranquillity. Careful attention has been paid to each and every detail of the spa's design and layout. Soothing colours mix with rich organic textures and uncluttered design to create a mood of pure serenity.

Whispers of flowing water invite guests through majestic Indian teak doors into the spa's central courtyard. Here, with the seamless African sky as a ceiling, there's time to relax around a palatial heated pool and enjoy the sights and sounds of Africa.

Around the central courtyard are beautifully-appointed treatment rooms, a state-of-the-art gym, steam room, hot and cold African baths and bush casitas where guests enjoy their treatment or simply relax in complete privacy. §

Make contact
see directory page 72

A river runs
through it

Dawn over Royal Zambezi presents some of the best sunrises you will ever see

Zambia's first and only bush spa. Overlooking the Lower Zambezi River, this tented 24-bed lodge shelters under a shaded canopy of huge indigenous trees. Its minimalist design exudes an air of complete peace, tranquillity and balance: the ultimate refuge to restore mind, body and spirit.

THE INVITING AROMA of burning scented candles fill the air from the spa's two beautifully-appointed treatment rooms set around the central courtyard. Their attentive team of qualified therapists provide guests with a wide variety of massages, facials and many other therapeutic and beauty skin care treatments.

The use of local indigenous ingredients from the African bush further emphasise the spa's natural beauty and enchantment. Guests are invited to use the energizing steam room, cooling plunge pool and outdoor jacuzzi with its breathtaking vista across the river – the perfect way to while away lazy afternoons. Spa body treatments include ancient hot stone massages and modern exfoliating wraps, treatments designed to detoxify the body, calm the mind and rejuvenate the skin. All treatments begin with a thorough consultation to assess any individual concerns to give the most appropriate facial treatment, leaving you with refreshed, smooth skin.

The Royal Zambezi Lodge Bush Spa takes the caring of your hands and feet to a whole new level – a necessity when on safari. Professional technicians pride themselves on giving you the best service possible.

There is also the beautifully appointed open lounge area; sip fresh juices while taking in the remarkable sights and sounds of the resident flora and fauna.

Dawn over Royal Zambezi presents some of the best sunrises you will ever see, casting a scarlet and golden glow over this great river. Watch wildlife browsing on the islands in harmony with the dawn chorus from countless birds and crickets. Elephant are often seen in camp in search of the succulent pods from the Winterthorn (Acacia Albida) or Tamarind trees.

Game drives in the Lower Zambezi National park, guided game walks, and boating, fishing and canoeing on the Zambezi can all be arranged. §

Make contact
see directory page 92

41:

Adventure in harmony
with Maasai warriors

This exclusive deluxe Kenyan game lodge is set in a remote valley in a conservation area bordering the Maasai Mara National Reserve. Owner-hosted, Saruni offers a new concept: the thrill of a real adventure lived in harmony with the Maasai warriors, coupled with high standards of style, comfort and a world-class spa experience.

Game drives and games walks are led by professional Maasai warriors

THE MOUNTAINS, ON THE WESTERN EDGE of the Maasai Mara, are the final destination for the famous Great Migration from July to October, which adds literally millions of animals to the resident herds. Guests will discover the beauty and skills of the Maasai people on one of the many game drives, game walks, bird-watching and hiking expeditions and cultural visits to the Maasai villages.

True bush spa
In collaboration with Grand Hotel des Iles Borromees (Stresa, Italy) and its world-famous spa – Centro Benessere Stresa, Saruni runs the Maasai Wellbeing Space. Guests can relax after a Maasai Mara safari in the most serene environment, enjoying massage and wellness treatments under the supervision of highly-trained staff. It's a private cottage hidden in the valley's olive and cedar forest and devoted to the use of local plants for beauty and relaxation treatments.

Game
The Maasai Mara is considered the jewel of African wildlife, nowhere on the continent can you find the same abundance and variety of wild animals. The lodge is located in one of the prime areas for ornithologists and hundreds of different species have been recorded. §

Make contact
see directory page 92

43:

An unforgettable
romantic getaway

Superbly situated close to the excellent game viewing areas of the private Welgevonden Game Reserve, five-star Shibula lodge hugs the banks of a scenic river with magnificent views of the overhanging cliffs where the resident baboon troop entertain guests.

Dine in an intimate wine cellar, or enjoy starlight boma dinners

FETED BY INTERNATIONAL MAGAZINES Marie Claire and ELLE as one of the more romantic destinations in Africa, Shibula offers a truly African experience in all its untamed magnificence. This malaria-free reserve, where the big five – Lion, Rhino, Buffalo, Elephant and Leopard – roam, is home to an extraordinary diversity of plant and animal wildlife, and more than 350 species of birds.

Bush Spa

Shibula's internationally-trained therapists provide relaxing and rejuvenating treatments in the newly-renovated Bush Spa to the background of natural sounds and smells. Personal body treatments use indigenous base oil ingredients such as Marula and Baobab, Rooibos and Kalahari Watermelon. Taking your body on a sense safari! Three signature treatments provide a unique spa experience:

The *TheraNaka Avocado and Shea butter nugget massage* begins by relaxing to the rhythms of Africa as blocks of avocado and shea butter are placed on legs, chest and back. The butter melts with the body's temperature and a deep tissue massage combined with Shiatsu trigger points results in a soothing warmth, leaving the body relaxed and skin hydrated and nourished.

The *TheraNaka African Wood Massage* begins with gentle stretching before specially-designed "Swarthout dumbbells" pummel warm olive and shea butter drizzled into the back, legs and chest. Leaving you feeling relaxed and rejuvenated.

Then there is the *TheraNaka Ultra Deluxe Relaxation Massage* indulging the full body using *TheraNaka* body oils. A head and scalp massage completes the experience with a special rain stick to gently awaken mind and body.

Cuisine

Dine in an intimate wine cellar, or enjoy starlight boma dinners, with traditional potjiekos and other gourmet dishes. Entertained by the excellent Shibula singers and dancers. 8

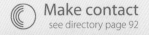

Make contact
see directory page 92

DESTINATION SPA

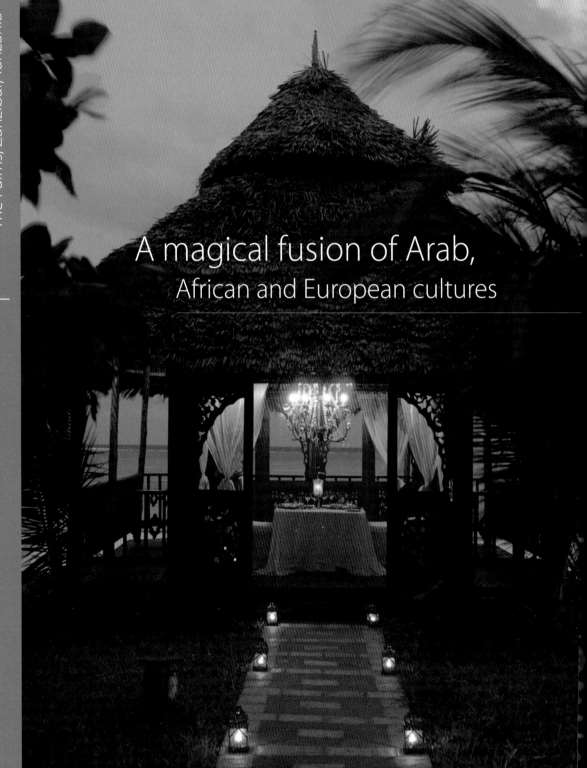

A magical fusion of Arab,
African and European cultures

Zanzibar is a magical island where the fusion of Arab, African and European cultures has created a unique pace of life, style of cuisine and colourful tapestry of architecture. Its combination of heritage, myth and magic is unrivalled anywhere else in the world.

Breezes Beach Club and Spa

Breezes is the perfect choice for those in search of a romantic getaway and wonderful spa experience with an exotic twist. Amid beautiful tropical landscaped gardens on a pristine, peaceful beach on Zanzibar's East Coast, Breezes Beach Club and Spa is famous for its attention to detail, intimate private dining and inspired Zanzibar deco. Stunning carvings, glistening brass and rich fabrics create an elegant and unique atmosphere.

Stunning carvings, glistening brass and rich fabrics create an elegant and unique atmosphere

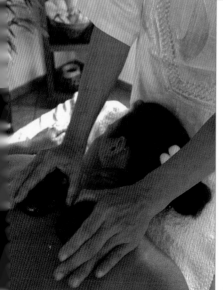

The Frangipani Spa reflects a sophisticated Swahili style enhanced with candlelight and spice-scented aromas. Located in whispering tropical gardens the spa offers world-class facilities and a selection of health and beauty treatments as well as specialised massage techniques including the renowned Thai Massage.

Their Sultan's Table is an exotic restaurant set on stilts with a beautiful view of the sea.

The Palms Zanzibar

On the South Eastern coast of this exotic island The Palms Zanzibar combines effortless elegance with Zanzibari sophistication. An oasis of rustling coconut palms, The Palms Zanzibar is a stunning hideaway for the discerning traveller. The collection of only six beautifully designed villas offer luxurious comfort as white powder sand and the warm waves of the Indian Ocean wash away stress and heal the spirit and stimulate the senses.

The Palms Zanzibar's Sanctuary Spa and the nearby Frangipani Spa conspire to offer a sophisticated menu of spa treats and rituals. §

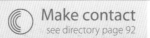

Seduction and
indulgence of the soul

Since its inception Fairlawns Spa has garnered a loyal following from all over the world. Combining age-old Asian healing traditions with natural tropical settings, the Fairlawns Spa aims to reacquaint guests with the lush beauty and quietude of Mother Nature.

Melt away knots, tension and stress while promoting positive energy flow

EMBRACING THE TIMELESS SENSATIONS of peace and tranquillity, Fairlawns seduces you into a world of relaxation, soothed by the gentle caress of soft music and fragrant oils. It is ideally situated, being so close to Sandton City, to treat stress-related symptoms, emotional tension, tension headaches, neck and shoulder spasms, jetlag, insomnia and a variety of other ailments. You are not spending on yourself, you are investing in yourself.

Holistic Sanctuary

Fairlawns is designed to be a holistic sanctuary – Balinese style. With the emphasis on personal service and a combination of Eastern and Western philosophies, innovative signature treatments and rituals, Fairlawns Spa radiates a warm and homely ambience set in beautiful surroundings offering peace, tranquillity and comfort. Intimate retreats are designed to blend romance and serenity with exotic sensuality and Fairlawns has fused ancient philosophies, beliefs and wisdoms with modern products, Eastern recipes and fresh, natural ingredients.

Current treatments include Hydro Active Mineral Salt Scrubs, Swedish and Aromatherapy as well as Indian head and scalp massage. The signature massage is the Harmony Four Hands Massage, where the expert hands of two skilled therapists simultaneously massage your body from head to toe.

Hot Stone Therapy is widely known for its deeply relaxing benefits employing a technique using smooth, heated basalt stones, which are placed on specific acupressure points on the body to melt away knots, tension and stress and promote a positive energy flow and greater sense of balance. Fairlawns Spa is one of the first to offer the unique Elemis Spa treatments recently launched in South Africa using a menu approach to treatments whereby clients select various elements of the spa packages. The Fairlawns Spa mission is to give each person who graces the spa a sublime sensory experience. §

Balance
is the key

A 5-star boutique hotel with a luxury spa, Fordoun was awarded the accolade of "Best Destination Spa" in 2006. Fordoun is committed to offering guests the freedom to structure their spa experience in a way that suits their individual needs.

FORDOUN IS SET IN THE FAMOUS KWAZULU-NATAL Midlands, and is uniquely designed with state-of-the-art facilities. All therapists at Fordoun undergo specific training to enhance the spa experience through understanding the principles of energy balancing and stress relief.

Owner, Jon Bates, who was recently awarded a Spa Ambassador award, believes that variety and personalised attention are more appropriate than strict regimes. The philosophy of the spa is built around balancing energy and empowering guests to understand the importance of physical, mental, emotional and spiritual balance.

Guests are empowered to understand the importance of physical, mental, emotional and spiritual balance

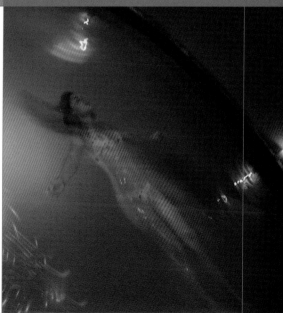

Enabling them to be more efficient in life, live happier lives and deal with all that life throws at them.

According to their physical and spiritual needs, guests can choose from a comprehensive range of beauty and wellness treatments, including sessions with the spa manager, lifestyle coach, and a Reiki master.

African touch

Well-known ethno-botanist and spiritual sangoma, Dr Elliot Ndlovu, is on hand to offer assistance using traditional African herbs and plants as well as consultations of a more spiritual nature. The Zulu Centre, with two treatment rooms and Dr. Ndlovu's consulting room is set in a garden of over 140 species of traditional healing plants. Spa treatments and products range from the leading international Elemis range to the natural African Ndlovu healing plant extracts.

The hotel has been 5-Star rated and its Skye restaurant offers healthy, hormone free and organic options to cater for both the dieter and the decadent. The emphasis is on relishing the moment and relaxing rather than starving and dieting although Fordoun's nutritionist will develop a healthy eating programme for individuals. §

A private
island home

In the Seychelles, four degrees below the equator, this private Island Paradise is just three square kilometres and boasts seven fine sandy beaches, a tropical jungle, fruit and vegetable plantations and a sanctuary for rare animals and birds.

LAPPED BY THE WARM INDIAN OCEAN, the island is private to Frégate guests only and the voluntary limitation to 16 private villas, restricts the number of guests at any one time to a maximum of 40. Making this the ideal refuge for the discerning traveller, ensuring the feeling of a rare tropical paradise island experience.

In the tranquil and spectacular natural surroundings of the Rock Spa and Sanctuary we offer an exclusive range of health and beauty therapies that are as unique and exotic as the island itself. Pamper and spoil your body, rejuvenate your spirit and restore your inner harmony with the renewed vitality that will stay with you long after you leave Frégate Island Private.

Four cliff-top treatment rooms are named after the elements in our native French Creole (Soley) sun, (Lesyel) sky, (Delo) water and (Ros) rock. Gathered together are the finest holistic therapies in the world, drawn from many different cultures and healing techniques providing a harmonious sensory experience.

For these as well as our own Frégate Signature Therapies, we rely on the abundance of natural ingredients that grow organically on the island – such as star fruit, frangipani, vanilla orchid, bread fruit, jasmine, papaya, avocado, ginger coconut mint lemon grass and ylang ylang.

Beginning with an aromatic flower footbath, that awakens the senses and allows you to enter a world of relaxation, our treatments are based upon the freshest seasonal fruit, flowers, aromatic leaves and spice available on the island. You can even select your own ingredients and have them ground in a pestle and mortar at the on-site apothecary. §

For most treatments and our own Frégate Signature therapies, we rely on the abundance of natural ingredients that grow organically on the island

Make contact
see directory page 92

Romance and high drama
take centre-stage

One of the most enchanting, romantic and eccentric retreats on the continent, Illyria House is a Shakespearian fantasy. A noble estate layered with the most fascinating antiques and 17th century tapestries.

If music be the food of love, play on

William Shakespeare

EXPERIENCE THE INTIMATE AMBIENCE of an aristocratic villa set in tranquil gardens. The serene beauty of Illyria House has always been an irresistible attraction to all lovers of fine things. Against the backdrop of classical music, an enchanting colonial lifestyle – complete with white-gloved butlers – unfolds.

Illyria House is highly appreciated by the discerning traveller for its charm, exquisite cuisine, exclusivity, luxury and unrivalled personalised service. Intimate pre-dinner soirees by world class musicians are enjoyed by guests.

Outdoor experiences, including a variety of activities such as golf, horse riding, tennis and hiking can be arranged. More classical pursuits such as picnics in the botanical gardens and visits to the State Theatre and Pretoria Art Museum, are a must.

Charming Spa

The newly-renovated Aquarius Wellness Spa is no less charming, romantic and inviting with exceptional attention to the smallest detail. A unique feature of the spa is a large open-air Jacuzzi bath where you can relax under the blue skies or memorise the South African stars at night.

Guests can enjoy treatments in the garden, or in the privacy of their own room. Manicures, pedicures, facials, massages and hairdressers can also be provided. §

A place to just be

Set beneath the towering amphitheatre of the Franschhoek mountains, is the most glorious of Cape destination spas, where a sensory experience, complete well-being and pure indulgence awaits.

Immerse yourself in the mysteries of unique fragrances – ginger, cinnamon and orange, creating a refreshing magical ambience

THE CAMELOT SPA AT LE FRANSCHHOEK is a true Destination Spa, combining traditional and scientific approaches to wellness and spa therapy in tranquillity, inspired by the mountains that surround it. Guests at the new Le Franschhoek Hotel have the most admired view across this passionate terroir – from its jumble of spiky, cathedral-like mountains to verdant rolling vignerons – making Le Franschhoek Hotel the most romantic of Cape Wineland getaways, with wellness and the good life at its core.

Relaxation and restoration await at the luxurious Camelot Spa. Immerse yourself in the mysteries of unique fragrances – ginger, cinnamon and orange, creating a refreshing magical ambience. In its treatments, Camelot uses the exclusive French marine spa product, Thalgo that – in harnessing the experience and mastery of the sea – is the undisputed leader at the forefront of International Spa Therapy.

Innovative signature treatments range from Eastern Herbal Massage to Thalgo Slim 'n Sculpt and combine with unique spa elements like the private liquid-sound flotation room (with sound in the water and a starry ceiling to enhance the experience). Try the "Moulin Rouge" colour-therapy room (where you will have your treatment while bathed in the chromo-therapeutic benefits of colour); or the marine hydrotherapy treatments; an aromatic herbal sauna; Swiss shower (experience steam along with thin jets of water); and a deluxe double treatment suite. There is even a private outdoor massage garden where you can enjoy a moonlight massage. The relaxing pause room and meditation area peer out onto a private courtyard where delicious health meals are served.

Apart from the exquisite Camelot Spa, Le Franschhoek Hotel's facilities also include the innovative al fresco Le Verger Restaurant, picnics to neighbouring farms, a sparkling swimming pool, tennis court, ballroom, two conference rooms, and a genuine cellar serving award-winning local wines. §

Make contact
see directory page 92

The ultimate escape

from the mundane

The award-winning Spa, Ananda in the Himalayas, now offers Shanti Ananda Maurice, a Destination Spa in Mauritius; a blissful Mauritian experience combined with a pathway to vitality through the union of body, mind and soul.

THE ANANDA SPA EXPERIENCE is the ultimate escape from the mundane to the spiritual, spread over 36 acres of tropical gardens with breathtaking views of lush hills and the crystal clear turquoise waters of the Indian Ocean.

Shanti Ananda's Spa is spread over 50,000 square feet and surrounded by water features. It offers an extensive menu of body and beauty treatments integrating traditional Indian systems of Ayurveda and Yoga with Thalassotherapy and contemporary International Spa Treatments.

An experienced team of Ayurvedic physicians, spa therapists and personal trainers are on hand and their combined expertise provides guidance towards healthier lifestyle changes. The spa offers a complete range of ESPA body and beauty treatments, a beauty and hair salon, boutique and a salt-water pool for Watsu treatments.

Yoga at Shanti Ananda is traditional from the roots of Hatha yoga with adaptations to suit individual needs. It is a disciplined science encompassing all aspects of life and assists in restoring perfect health, leading from one consciousness to super-consciousness, resulting in the achievement of 'Sat Chitt Ananda', or 'eternal bliss', the ultimate aim of Yoga.

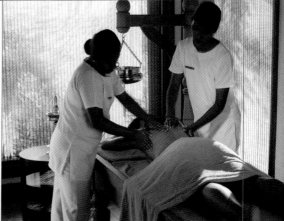

Shanti Ananda Spa cuisine

Spa cuisine at Shanti Ananda is based on the 5,000-year-old medical science of Ayurveda, based on the importance of the right food depending on one's body-type; Vata, Pita and Kapha. The food at Shanti Ananda is an eclectic and wholesome combination that eventually leads to perfect health, the natural way. §

Ananda techniques are grounded in ancient Indian traditions yet simply taught and immediately practical for modern needs

Make contact
see directory page 92

The scent of roses
and old world charm

Nestled in a natural forest and plantations of mangoes, litchis, macadamia nuts and roses, Summerfields River Lodge and Rose Spa is a luxury tented lodge, unique wellness spa and gourmet restaurant.

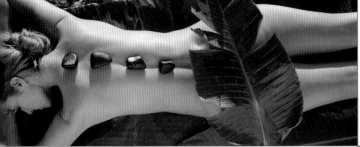

Roses are everywhere. Rose essences leave the skin hydrated, balanced, smooth and radiant.

THIS IS A MOST ENCHANTING PLACE TO LAY low from the pressures of urban life, a retreat of intriguing charm defined by the bygone romance of percale linen in luxuriously-appointed tented suites.

Set beneath a canopy of Jackalberry and Tambotie trees, these tented suites have outdoor baths and showers and are open to the sounds of cascading water. Service is genteel and a bath butler is on hand to run an aroma bath before retiring.

Rose spa

Roses are everywhere. Renowned for its skin enhancing properties – to nourish, calm, balance and control the skin's needs – rose essences leave the skin hydrated, balanced, smooth and radiant. Unashamedly indulgent and immediately healing, the Spa boasts a variety of signature treatments, a unique outdoor hydrotherapy meander and rose quartz steam shower, reached by a reflexology walk. Take a treatment beside the tranquil Sabie River while the resident crocodile looks on from his sun-drenched riverine rock. Summerfields uses Thalgo, the prestigious French spa, beauty and wellness range.

Cuisine

Rose essence is also used in the gourmet Summerfields Kitchen (desserts especially) fashioned by chef Lienkie Erasmus, renowned on SA's gourmet circuit for her country-chic style; embracing local produce with fresh herb garden pickings and homemade chutneys, mayonnaise and bread.

MUST TRY: Escape urban stress by being whisked off celebrity-style in the comfort of Summerfields' own private aircraft. Take a game drive (Kruger National Park is 10km away) or try the tree canopy aerial walkway. ⚘

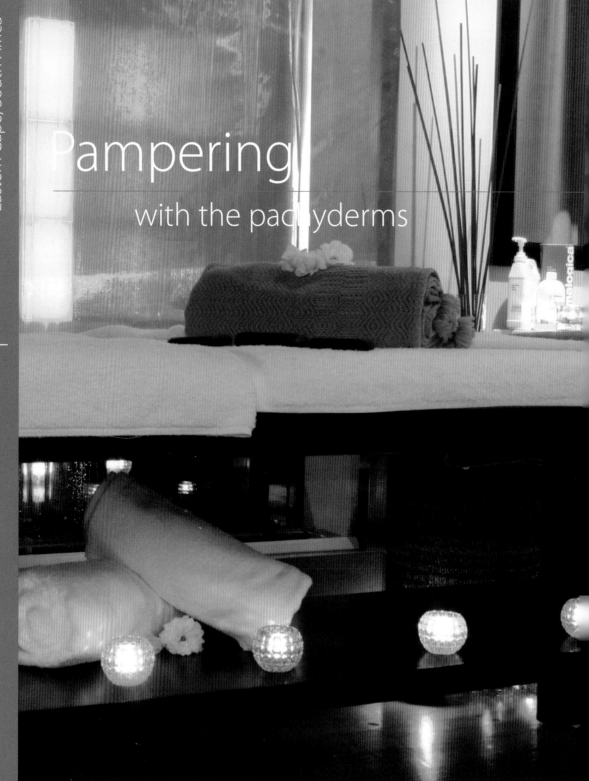

Pampering

with the pachyderms

On the doorstep of Addo Elephant Park, Woodall Country House and Spa is tucked away on a peaceful citrus farm where the trees bear fruit all winter and blossoms scent the air in spring. A full range of facial and body treatments will leave you feeling completely pampered.

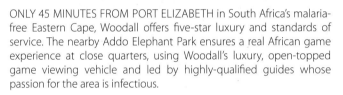

A full range of facial and body treatments will leave you feeling pampered, relaxed and rejuvenated

ONLY 45 MINUTES FROM PORT ELIZABETH in South Africa's malaria-free Eastern Cape, Woodall offers five-star luxury and standards of service. The nearby Addo Elephant Park ensures a real African game experience at close quarters, using Woodall's luxury, open-topped game viewing vehicle and led by highly-qualified guides whose passion for the area is infectious.

The Spa

The Woodall Spa, a sanctuary for relaxation, personal rejuvenation and serious pampering flows onto a full-size pool, fringed with palms and a gushing waterfall. Facilities include massage and therapy room, couples therapy room, nail bar, relaxation area, steam room, sauna, hydrotherapy bath and spacious double showers. The fully-equipped gym offers cardiovascular and strength training facilities.

A full range of facial and body treatments will leave you feeling pampered, relaxed and rejuvenated. Individual skin types are fully analysed prior to skincare treatments, leaving you with perfectly hydrated, relaxed and radiant skin. All skincare treatments use the excellent Dermalogica range. Massage therapies include Swedish, Aromatherapy, Foot Massages, and Hot Stone Massages that melt the tension from each and every tired muscle.

Body exfoliations with aromatherapy and Mineral Salts that lift dead skin cells and Hydrotherapy and Sea Mud Packs that detoxify, refresh and relax your body, are all recommended. Woodall's special Jet Lag treatments will alleviate any negative symptoms of jet travel so you can more comfortably enjoy the full benefit of your stay.

Spa Cuisine

Delicious gourmet spa cuisine – low in kilojoules without skimping on flavour – can be enjoyed overlooking the water sanctuary. Dinners are gourmet six-course set menus featuring local cuisine and the kitchen provides for various dietary requirements on request.

Complementing the menu is the award-winning wine cellar. §

Special experiences for special people

True to the Zorgvliet spirit of service excellence and the brand promise of "special experiences for special people", Zorgvliet Spa provides guests with an array of beauty and relaxation treatments at all Zorgvliet Portfolio destinations. Guests are pampered with a variety of body and skin treatments such as wraps, scrubs, anti stress massages, as well as detoxifying and slimming treatments – set in unique environments surrounded by the natural beauty of nature.

Take advantage of an outside treatment to soak up the serene atmosphere of the African bush

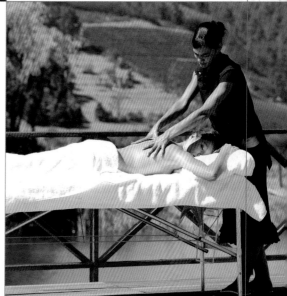

ZORGVLIET SPA situated at Zorgvliet Vineyard Lodge & Spa near Stellenbosch, offers an array of professional body care, overall well-being and facial care solutions. Whether you prefer a relaxing back, neck and shoulder massage or need purification through a hydrating skin treatment, Zorgvliet will ensure that you are pampered.

Zorgvliet Spa at Ka'Ingo Private Reserve and Spa in the Waterberg area is a good spot for wellness in the wilderness. The treatments on offer at this luxury bush spa range from basic facials to specialised body treatments including body wraps and Indian head massages. Take advantage of an outside treatment and soak-up the serene atmosphere in the heart of the African bush. After an hour or two of this kind of pampering you will soon forget all the stresses related to fast paced city life.

Enjoy the ultimate pampering on the banks of the Vaal River – visit Zorgvliet Spa situated at the Riviera on Vaal Hotel and Country Club. Relax and rejuvenate both body and mind in a tranquil environment complete with a panoramic view of the Vaal River.

The 4th edition to the Zorgvliet Spa stable will be opening soon at Protea Hotel King George in George. ❀

Make contact
see directory page 92

DAY SPA

To live life

and savour time

Angsana Spa takes its name from the exotic Angsana tree, a statuesque tree found in the tropical rainforests of Asia. The glorious Angsana beholds the maxim to live life and savour time as it passes inexorably. Cherish relaxing moments at this ultra-professional spa.

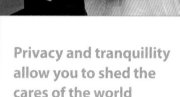

Privacy and tranquillity allow you to shed the cares of the world

Tranquil charm

The privacy and tranquillity of each Angsana Spa retreat allows you to shed the cares of the world and rediscover essential sensory pleasures. The historic Vineyard Hotel is well known for its quiet charm and beautiful setting in the heart of picturesque Cape Town. Its sprawling, landscaped gardens are flanked by the magnificent Table Mountain, Kirstenbosch National Botanical Gardens and Liesbeeck River, creating a spectacular retreat.

Angsana Spa adds a touch of indulgent Asian pampering to this gem of a hotel. It has ten lavish spa rooms, as well as a specially-equipped Rainmist room to add cache to this special hideaway for blissful rejuvenation

Angsana Spa treatments are designed with only one purpose in mind – to ensure that when clients leave they are naturally refreshed and revitalised. Their signature Ayurvedic Rainmist spa treatment is particularly recommended as a truly luxurious revitaliser that will soothe any body to sheer heaven!

Sanctuary for the inner self

The self needs solitude, space and peace to recharge its batteries. Angsana Spa is designed to be a sanctuary for the inner self, to refresh and rejuvenate your spirit as well as your physical being.

Privacy and tranquillity allow you to shed the cares of the world while allowing expert therapists to pamper your body and mind, with invigorating treatments. Angsana encourages you to experience the spa with a loved one and rediscover essential sensory pleasures – from the pleasure of touch to the aroma of exotic oils like rosemary, lavender, jasmine and frangipani wafting through the air. §

Country pleasures,
minutes from the city

This unique setting on a 6-acre country estate just 3km from Fourways Mall helps you switch off from urban stress as you step out of the city into a country haven of peace and heavenly tranquillity.

Experience the beauty of a Highveld sunset on the terrace after a very special relaxing days

THE OPEN BODY SENSE ENVIRONMENT contrasts sharply with the confines of large clinical buildings or pokey treatment rooms. Experience the beauty of a Highveld sunset on the terrace after an unbelievably relaxing day. Unwind and revitalise in a pleasant, relaxed environment and leave with a sense of complete wellbeing. Professional therapists are there to pamper you no matter which treatment or package you choose. All rejuvenating packages include either breakfast or lunch or both for full day retreats.

Day packages

Body Sense Day Spa offers a range of specialised packages tailored to individual needs and staff will go out of their way to ensure that everyone is catered for.

These include Full Day revitalisation and Half-Day stress relief packages to offer a refreshing energising boost to stressed executives. There are also numerous special "event" packages that range from a Mother and Daughter's day, anniversary and special birthday packages. Hen parties have become extremely popular where friends get together over a Champagne breakfast or afternoon tea and enjoy a private venue with treatments all to themselves. Its interesting that incentive or thank you spa packages as a reward for sales staff have become more valued than a lunch or dinner at a restaurant.

Private groups receive personal attention without feeling they're on a conveyor belt. Body Sense stocks Environ, Guinot, Lilian Terry Aromeopathic Oils and Essie Nailcare Products offering each client an opportunity to achieve absolute relaxation on a budget.

A personal spa itinerary can be designed to fit in with any request, including a limousine drive to the spa for that special occasion. The lunch menu too can be tailored to any taste. Accommodation can be arranged upon request and a chauffer service is available within a 15km radius. §

Space and time to breathe easily

Bordered by rich forest and farmland, with a meandering stream running through the property, the Brookdale estate consists of the main Health Hydro with accommodation and treatment facilities, and a separate Day Spa. Guest suites are bordered by garden courtyards and the whole environment is conducive to relaxation and tranquillity.

BROOKDALE BOASTS AN UNUSUALLY high ratio of qualified staff to guests, ensuring the personal attention and exclusivity which has become a hallmark. On arrival, a consultant meets each guest to ascertain their health, level of fitness personal preferences and to advise suitable treatments, exercise and nutrition.

A realistic approach to embracing a balanced lifestyle

Brookdale Health Hydro focuses on re-establishing healthy lifestyles and restoring mental wellbeing where stressful living has taken a toll. While the approach is a personal one, it allows guests space and time to breathe freely. The realistic Nutri-fit Program devised by exercise physiologist, Rob Cowling, has been scientifically developed into a unique composite approach based on healthy eating, moderate exercise and stress management.

At Brookdale, deep relaxation is at the core of de-stressing. Experienced therapists are focused on achieving this with a wide range of luxurious treatments using only reputable products from established brands such as Guinot, Babor, Ahava, Clarins, OPI, Paul Mitchell and Environ.

The indoor wet area features a stunning heated pool surrounded by a sandstone terrace, sunny conservatory, a jacuzzi, sauna and steam rooms and a health bar. In addition, the hydro also offers a mosaic steam room, sauna, hydrotherapy baths, a fully equipped gym and a studio with Pilates, Yoga and Guided Relaxation classes.

Brookdale is a place to retreat from the world, relax the spirit and refresh the soul. §

A sense of soul

IMBUED WITH AN ESSENTIAL SENSE OF SOUL, Camelot embraces the three pillars of spa wisdom: rest, relax and revitalise. Its vision for the future of wellness is based on past wisdoms and the name Camelot is now synonymous with the term "spa culture".

WALK INTO ANY CAMELOT SPA and you are immersed in an holistic warmth and blissful serenity derived from the wisdom of balance. Its spas regularly host such red carpet stars as Charlize Theron, Sean Connery, Naomi Campbell and others who pop in to pep up. Camelot Spas emanate a certain presence that shines from within – a place where the path to beauty and ultimate wellness begins. In an on-going evolution, Camelot has pioneered a new generation of therapies focussed on natural plant and marine technology to promote a healthy body and state of mind, honouring spirit and unwinding emotions.

Table Bay Hotel

Royal Swazi

Camelot Spas emanate a certain presence that shines from within – a place where the path to beauty and ultimate wellness begins

Table Bay
Located on Cape Town's Victoria & Alfred Waterfront against the back-drop of Table Mountain, Camelot Spa at The Table Bay Hotel boasts five treatment rooms and two specialist rooms for Vichy Shower and Aromatherapy. The spa offers the latest technology and a focused range of global treatments; from Swedish connective-tissue treatment to Ayurvedic techniques from ancient India.

Royal Swazi
The Royal Kingdom of Swaziland has a history of tradition and culture that pervades the land and infuses the Valleys. The Royal Swazi Sun nestles in the Ezulwini Valley and royal custom reigns.

The Camelot Spa at the Royal Swazi is set in tranquil gardens overlooking the golf course with tremendous mountain views. It is a haven of peace and gentle efficiency. There are eight full-time therapists offering a variety of treats and rituals. Back massage, foot and hand treatments, exfoliation, aromatherapy massage… the spa menu is broad and even includes the popular Golfer's Reviving treatment.

With over 12 spas in the most beguiling locations – from beach to bush, winelands and glamorous city locales – Camelot Spa is at the forefront of stylish spa culture. §

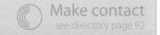

The first Clarins Skin Spa in Africa

On the 1 March 2005 Clarins South Africa became part of the global family when it opened the first Clarins Institut in Africa at its headquarters in Johannesburg. Now two years later they are changing the name to the Clarins Skin Spa. A sanctuary in the city which offers a retreat where you can nurture mind, body and soul.

"Take time to experience a Clarins treatment: a moment of absolute well-being, the pleasure of the senses and renewed beauty"
– *Jacques Courtin-Clarins*

DESIGNED BY AN EXPERT TEAM OF CLARINS architects in Paris, this world-class state-of-the-art centre offers six rooms, which include a men's specific area and couples room. In addition to this, the Spa offers full wet facilities including Vichy Shower room and Spa Bath. A comprehensive range of treatments include the spa experience, Clarins pro-face and pro-body treatments, pre- and post-natal treatments, men's treatments and finishing touches. The Clarins Skin Spa is a sensory experience that addresses the way you look and feel.

The Clarins Touch

At the Clarins Skin Spa, all the treatments are based on the Clarins Touch. This unique and professional method involves over 80 intricate movements developed by the founder of Clarins, Jacques Courtin-Clarins.

Highly trained and professional therapists use different rhythmic strokes to stimulate lymph drainage, boost circulation and restore balance to encourage wellbeing in the body and mind. No Appliance or machine is as sensitive or dexterous as the hands of a Clarins-trained therapist. §

For added convenience and pleasure, Clarins Skin Spa, South Africa, is open Monday to Thursday from 08h00 to 19h00, Friday and Saturday from 08h00 to 17h00 and Sunday from 09h00 to 14h00, allowing clients to unwind straight after work or at their leisure over the weekend.

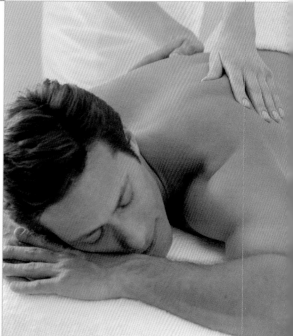

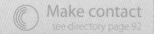

Make contact
see directory page 92

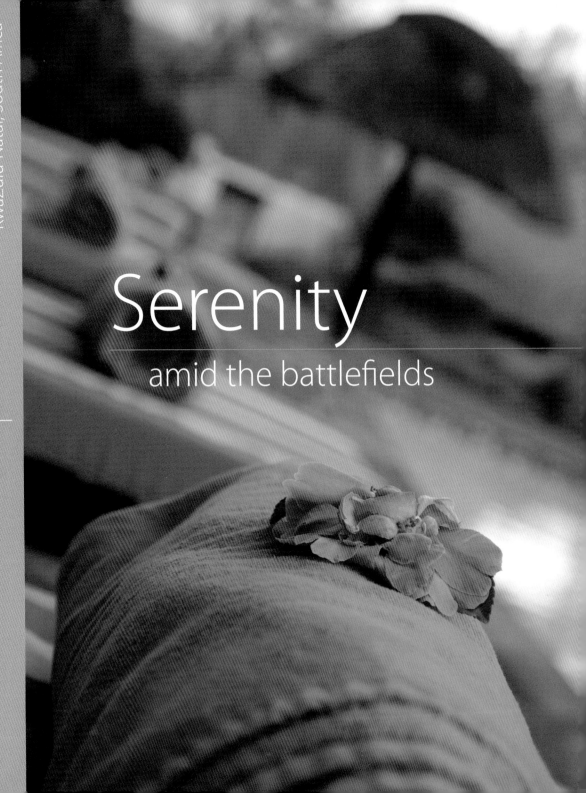

Serenity

amid the battlefields

Surrounded by battlefields steeped in the history of Zulu warriors, Granny Mouse is a legendary destination. Set in the heart of the KwaZulu-Natal Midlands, at the gateway to the Drakensberg foothills, Granny Mouse Country House, is an exquisite Hotel, gourmet restaurant, and now boasts a newly-opened Wellness Centre and Spa.

GRANNY MOUSE IS THE PERFECT country venue for weddings, conferences or a honeymoon getaway offering upmarket accommodation on a Bed & Breakfast basis. Golf courses, fly-fishing and birding are on the doorstep.

This popular retreat now has one of the most complete and indulgent all-round packages in KwaZulu-Natal

Yet it's newly-opened luxury spa facility offers the pleasure of a Hot Stone Massage as one of the many treatments at the hands of expert therapists.

This retreat is now one of the most complete and indulgent all-round packages in KwaZulu-Natal. The new spa offers a full range of massage and skin treatments, as well as a state of the art steam room, Jacuzzi and hydrotherapies. Using Algologie, Dermalogica, Lilian and Terry International and O.P.I for you to indulge yourself.

Gourmet cuisine

Its gourmet lunches and dinners are renowned throughout the Caversham Valley. Views of the Lions River are taken in while enjoying one of the superb wines from the hotel's underground wine cellar. 8

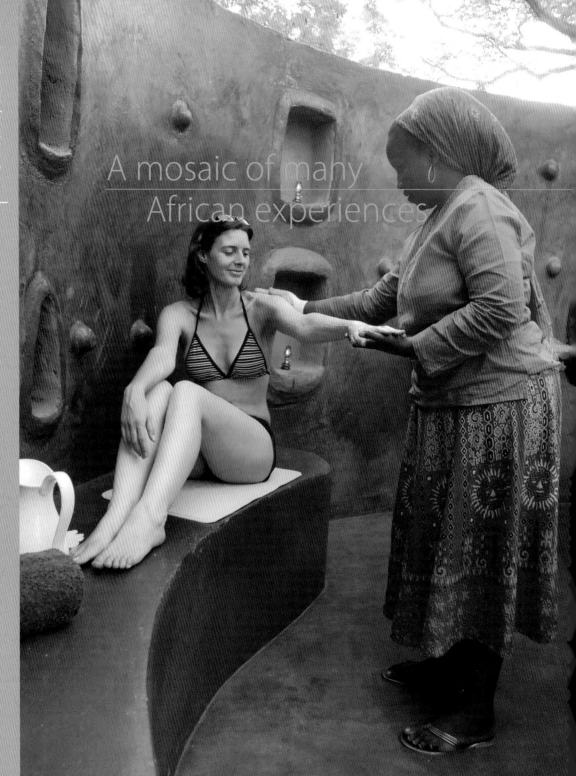

A mosaic of many
African experiences

Kiasoma is a heavenly retreat that seeks to instill the essence and spirit of the new millennium in the lives of those who spend time there. A truly African experience, Kiasoma thrives on proximity to mother earth and all its wonderful offerings, physical and spiritual.

Kiasoma is an unusual and eclectic mix of haven, retreat and wellness centre offering surprising variety of treatments

SOUTH AFRICA IS A MOSAIK OF DIFFERENT CULTURES, our planet is a mosaik of humanity and consequently the retreat is named Kiasoma – for the words A MOSAIK read as Kiasoma when the letters are reversed. This explains the quaint eccentricity of this powerfully spiritual retreat that is so much more than a spa.

Kiasoma is an unusual and eclectic mix of haven, retreat and wellness centre. You can get involved in courses and workshops for a number of self improvements or indulge in the superior spa experience. This distinctly African spa offers a variety of treatments including Full Body Massage, Hot Stone Massage, Indian Head and Shoulders, Muti Mud Scrubs, Reiki, Kahuna Massage, Crystal Healing, Manicures, Pedicures and Facials.

Kiasoma offers art and healing weekends, and will structure a weekend to suit each individual.

There is a one hour, two hour, or three hour hiking trail at Kiasoma, that boasts over 350 species of birdlife. Another popular request is a photo-shoot weekend whereby a photography club will book in for a weekend of private photography..

Should you not want to experience any of the healing modalities or art lessons, you are welcome to stay in their self-catering or bed & breakfast cottages. Relax and enjoy the peace and tranquillity of this spectacular African retreat. §

Make contact
see directory page 92

The "original" African Day Spa

Mangwanani Private African Day Spa is situated in numerous locations around South Africa, from the serene bush surroundings at Hennops River Valley to treatment rooms nestled in a tranquil forest at Bashewa in Pretoria East. Visit Mangwanani Day Spa along the idyllic wine route at Zevenwacht in the Cape Winelands, or find it in the Entertainment Kingdom – Sibaya in KwaZulu Natal.

A rare experience of true African Indulgence where the touch of our forefathers still runs through the fingertips of our tribe

MANGWANANI IS A TRUE AFRICAN experience where the touch of our forefathers still runs through the fingertips of our tribe. Guests are transported to an African Inspired Oasis, where they are pampered and spoilt in real African Royal Tradition.

Mangwanani offers an ideal tranquil setting for guests to enjoy a day of sheer decadence, complete relaxation and de-stressing. There are a large variety of spa packages available to accommodate a diversity of clients' needs. Revitalisation treatments for men and women, corporate groups and private individuals are all taken care of.

Dressed in bright orange – the healing colour of Africa – Mangwanani staff greet guests with traditional singing and drumming, while the therapists use African oils, ochre, sugars, sands, herbs, spices, flowers, petals, barks and roots.

The Mangwanani Experience
Spa highlights include: UBUSO (Renewing African Facial Spa) but note that this is not a beauty facial, the accent is on relaxation; TLHAPISO the Full Body Cleansing – Gift of Nature); IZIMANGA (Full Body Massage – Heaven on Earth with a Blend of Essential Oils); MOLALA (Ancient Indian / North African Head Massage) with Sesame Oil; NEO MAOTO (Foot Gift) Traditional African Royal Foot Gift (from toes to knees) and NEO MATSOGO (Hand Gift) a Traditional African Royal Hand Gift (from fingers to elbows).

Mangwanani Spa is the ideal setting for complete relaxation. Champagne breakfasts, full buffet lunches with wine or full bar facilities are included in the day packages. Decadent treats such as imported chocolates, home made biscuits, beverages and snacks are available throughout the day. A stricter health programme can be arranged if required.

Our highly-trained therapists are ready and willing to help you on your journey, with treatments passed down through generations and moulded into sought after therapies. §

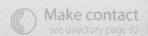

Make contact
see directory page 92

A warm, welcoming specialist salon

New in Johannesburg, MediSalon offers the unique concept of a high-tech anti-ageing and aesthetic clinic specialising in non-invasive plastic surgery. It is conveniently situated in Sandton for both local and international clientele.

MEDI SALON SPECIALISES IN NON-INVASIVE plastic surgery using laser, infra-red and ultrasound among other sophisticated cutting-edge non-invasive procedures. The specialist team at MediSalon are experts at dealing with a variety of treatments such as: facial rejuvenation, acne prevention and scarring, wrinkle reduction, hair removal, post-plastic surgery skin care, anti-ageing massage and facial, body contouring and firming, cellulite and slimming.

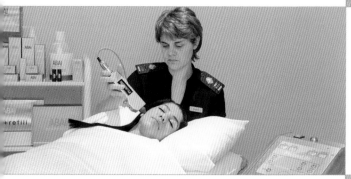

MediSalon's specialist staff are expert at performing a variety of treatments using the latest technology available

Despite the modern technology and medical techniques which can often be intimidating, the Salon is very professional, warm and welcoming; exceeding all expectations to make you feel comfortable at all times.

The Team
A committed, knowledgeable team of qualified medical staff, specialist nurses and beauty therapists are on hand to perform all treatments, in a sterile environment, adhering to the highest standards of quality and safety. The wellbeing and comfort of clients combined with consistent, tangible, effective results is the number one priority.

A free non-invasive consultation is offered to new clients without obligation and all treatment schedules are tailor-made to suit the client's specific requirements. MediSalon also offers patrons a complimentary selection of health foods and fresh juices free of charge from their delicious gourmet health bar to be enjoyed in the pause area in-between sessions or while recuperating.

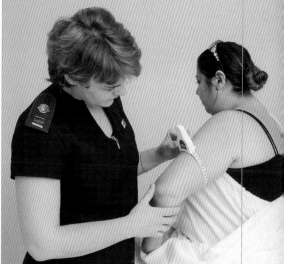

Make contact
see directory page 92

African tradition

with European flair

The Misty Hills Spa in the Country, overlooking the Kromdraai Valley, was conceived and designed as an African sanctuary. Guests are pampered in a serene environment that encourages relaxation and personal rejuvenation.

INDIGENOUS AFRICAN HERBS, FLOWERS and spices embody a natural approach to body and skin care, infusing ancient African beauty and health therapies with conventional treatments. The result is a range of exciting and innovative treatments that infuse traditional African and modern spa trends, from a unique African Muti Mud experience to the innovative Chocolate Decadence or Coffee Treatments.

European opulence combines with African inspiration in The Signature Room indulging the senses in total seclusion

Top spa

Consistently voted among the top spas in South Africa, Misty Hills focuses on qualified therapists delivering a quality experience that pampers the individual through an eclectic spectrum of treatments including Anti-stress massage, Kahuna massage, Aromatherapy and Reflexology through to advanced natural remedy skin care and water treatments.

Misty Hills' unique day spa experience caters for single treatments, half day or full day packages. Tailored individual and group packages are also available. Treatment rooms are set in a lush indigenous setting with cascading water features to soothe the senses. Guests are encouraged to make full use of the indigenous gardens, nude sun bathing area and indoor heated pool.

Signature treatments

These include, Kahuna; Bamboo massage and African Calabash massage, Baoula massage; African Rungu massage; Herbal massage; Morrocan massage; Polynesian massage; as well as a full menu of traditional spa treatments. §

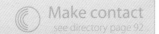

Make contact
see directory page 92

Affordable pampering

amid breathtaking scenery

Situated in the heart of the Magaliesberg Mountains, a mere 90 minutes from Johannesburg, Sparkling Health Spa promises affordable pampering without compromising luxury – supreme wellness amid breathtaking scenery.

THIS AWARD-WINNING SPA – VOTED "Stay Spa Of The Year" in 2006, is situated in the sub-tropical gardens of the Sparkling Waters Hotel and housed in a charming 750 m² thatched pavilion, providing the perfect haven to revitalise your mind, body and spirit. Sparkling Health Spa is the largest and most modern facility of its kind in the North West Province and, like Sparkling Waters Hotel, the Health Spa's mottos are "Value for Money, "Home from Home" and "Never say No."

Open-air treatments are done in a charming tented gazebo where clients are surrounded by exotic tropical gardens and a private meditation area. Treatments on offer include a wide selection of facials, massages, body treatments, wraps, reflexology pedicures and manicures.

Sparkling Health Spa operates as a day-and-stay spa, offering a selection of indulgent 1– 3 day packages. Whether you're a day or stay client, the expert therapists and staff will provide impeccable service. There is an indoor heated pool, small gym, steam bath, hydro-therapy room, double signature-treatment room, sun-bed and two-tier wooden sun deck, overlooking divine woods next to the Krom River and Tropical Jacuzzi garden.

Signature Highlights include
Theravine elite 3¹/₂ hour package
Start with a Pinotage, grape seed body-exfoliation, Red Grapeskin hydro-therapy treatment, vine full body massage and a Theravine facial.

Head to toe Organic 3-hour package
Start with an Apricot body polish, Rosemary-infused head massage, detoxifying Rooibos-and-Honey full-body massage with a peppermint Rooibos- and-honey hot stone foot treatment and pedicure. §

Whether you're a day or stay client, the expert therapists and staff will provide impeccable service

RESORT SPAS

DIANI REEF BEACH RESORT & SPA
P. O. Box 54776, Nairobi 00200, Kenya
(t): +254 020 3742657
(f): +254 020 3742647
E-mail: info@dianireef.com
www.dianireef.com

LA SULTANA MARRAKECH
403 Rue de la Kasbah, 40000 Marrakech
(t): +212 24 38 80 08
(f): +212 24 38 98 09
E-mail: reservation@lasultanahotels.com /
www.lasultanahotels.com

THE GIVENCHY SPA AT LE TOUESSROK
Trou d 'Eau Douce, Mauritius
(t): +230 402 7400
(f): +230 402 7500
E-mail: info@letouessrok.mu
www.letouessrokresort.com

PEZULA RESORT HOTEL & SPA
Eastern Head, Lagoonview Drive, Knysna, Sou
(t): +27 (0) 44 302 3313
(f): +27 (0) 44 384 1658
E-mail: hotel@pezula.com
www.pezula.com

PRESKÎL BEACH RESORT
Pointe Jerome, Mahebourg, Mauritius
(t): +230 604 1000
(f): +230 631 9603
E-mail: hotel@lepreskil.mu
www.lepreskil.com | www.relaisdeslodges.com

SERENA BEACH HOTEL & SPA
P.O. Box 90352, Mombasa, Kenya
(t): +254 (0) 41 5485721 or 041 3548771
(f): +254 (0) 41 5485453 or 041 3548775
E-mail: mombasa@serena.co.ke
www.serenahotels.com

SOFITEL IMPERIAL MAURITIUS
Wolmar, Flic en Flac, Mauritius
(t): +230 453 8700
(f): +230 453 8320
E-mail: H1144@accor.com
www.sofitel.com

TAJ EXOTICA RESORT & SPA, MALDI
P.O. Box 2117, South Male Atoll, Maldives
(t): +960 664 22 00
(f): +960 664 22 11
E-mail: exotica.maldives@tajhotels.com
www.tajhotels.com

TAJ EXOTICA RESORT & SPA, MAURITIUS
Wolmar, Flic en Flac, Mauritius
(t): +230 403 1500
(f): +230 453 5555
E-mail: exotica.mauritius@tajhotels.com
www.tajhotels.com

BUSH SPAS

ETALI SAFARI LODGE

221 Milner Street, Waterkloof, Pretoria
(t): +27 (0)12 346 0124 / +27 (0) 83 442 6557
(f): +27 (0)12 346 0163
E-mail: info@etalisafari.co.za
www.etalisafari.co.za

FALAZA GAME PARK & SPA

P.O. Box 13, Hluhluwe 3960, Zululand, South Africa
(t): +27 (0) 35 562 2319
(f): +27 (0) 35 562 2086
E-mail: resfalaz@telkomsa.net
www.falaza.co.za

GARONGA SAFARI CAMP

P.O. Box 737, Hoedspruit, 1380, South Africa
(t): +27 (0) 82 440 3522
(f): +27 (0)15 318 7902
E-mail: safari@garonga.com
www.garonga.com

PESTANA KRUGER LODGE

R507, Kruger National Park, Malelane Gate,
Mpumalanga, South Africa
(t): +27 (0) 13 790 2503
(f): +27 (0) 13 790 0280
E-mail: kruger.lodge@pestana.com
www.pestana.com

THE WATERS OF ROYAL MALEWANE BUSH SPA

Royal Malewane Private Safari Lodge, Avoca Road,
Hoedspruit, Limpopo, South Africa
(t): +27 15 793 0150
(f): +27 15 793 2879
E-mail: info@royalmalewane.com
www.royalmalewane.com

THE ROYAL ZAMBEZI LODGE BUSH SPA

P/Bag CH42, Lusaka, Zambia
(t): +260 1 261 265 / +260-979-486618
(f): +260 1 261 265
E-mail: royalzambezihq@iwayafrica.com
www.royalzambezilodge.com

SARUNI KENYA

Saruni is in the Maasai Mara ecosystem, Kenya
The coordinates are S 01° 08' 52.3" E 035° 17' 27.0"
(t): +254 502 2424
E-mail: riccardo@sarunicamp.com
www.sarunicamp.com

SHIBULA LODGE & BUSH SPA

Welgevonden Game Reserve, Vaalwater, Limpopo, South Africa
(t): +27 (0) 21 882 8206 / +27 (0) 82 788 5100
(f): +27 (0) 14 755 4916
E-mail: reservations@shibulalodge.co.za
www.shibulalodge.co.za

DESTINATION SPAS